Lamont Jackson

THE JOB INTERVIEW

AN EMPLOYERS PERSPECTIVE

YOUR GUIDE TO A BETTER INTERVIEW

VOLUME 2

By
LAMONT M. JACKSON

Emont Publishing
Books that empower, inform & motivate.

RALEIGH, NC

Library Commons
Georgian College
One Georgian Drive
Barrie, ON
L4M 3X9

Lamont Jackson

TEXT COPYRIGHT © 2014 Lamont Jackson

No part of this work may be reproduced, transcribed, or used in any form or by any means-graphic, or mechanical, including photocopying, recording, taping, Web distribution, or information storage and retrieval systems-without the prior written permission of the author & publisher. The only exception is by a reviewer, who may quote short excerpts in a review.

Emont Publishing
Lamont Jackson
P.O. Box 14387
Raleigh, NC. 27620

First Printing: January 2014
For more information go to:
  www.lamontjackson.com. Or www.emontpublishing.com

Lamont Jackson, 2014
"The Job Interview" an employer's perspective: A book by Lamont Jackson – 2nd ed.

Disclaimer
"The Job Interview" is a book written from an employer's perspective. It provides descriptions, purposes, situations and individual understandings of the actual interview process. This book is not intended as legal advice. Neither the author nor publisher is engaged in rendering legal advice. We are asked to speak with an attorney for legal advice. Because laws vary by state and are subject to change at the Federal level, neither the author nor publisher guarantees the accuracy of this information. Should you act based on this information, you do so at your sole risk. Neither the author nor publisher shall have any liability arising from your decision to act on this information.

ISBN 10: 0985944617
ISBN 13: 978-0-9859446-1-2

Cover and text design: Lamont Jackson

Emont Publishing, Inc. Books are available at special discounts for bulk purchases by corporations, institutions, and other organizations. For more information, contact us at orders@emontpublishing.com

Printed in the United States

Lamont Jackson

DEDICATION

This book is dedicated to Marie "Mommy" Buoncuore, thank you for being the mother my wife needed in a very fragile time in her life. We love you and would like to thank you for all that you do. I also dedicate this book to my two daughters LaShay and Lindsey for being beautiful, intelligent and loving and understanding that dad loves his girls more than he loves himself. You guys are my purpose in all that I do. Above all else, thank you to the love of my life, my wife, Wessie Jackson for being the most wonderful and supportive wife in the world. Thank you for understanding my ambitious nature. This one is for you.

Lamont Jackson

CONTENTS

INTRODUCTION	1
PART I	
AN INVITATION TO INTERVIEW	1
A Process of Elimination	6
Why Companies are so Selective	8
PART II	
PREPARING FOR THE INTERVIEW	10
Your Resume	11
Accurate Contact Information	13
Active Phone Numbers	14
Voice Mail	15
Create a Better Email Address	16
Know the Organization	18
What Do You Really Know About a Potential Employer?	18
When Was the Organization Established?	20
Any Changes in Board Members or Executive Staff Positions	20
Financial Information (Annual Report)	22
Is the Organization Is Unionized	23
How Many Members	24
Local Union Name	24
Union's Information, its Leadership and Policies and the Organization's Relationship with the Union?	24
Salary Range	25
Know the Position	26
Social Media	27
PART III	
THE INTERVIEW PROCESS	30
Arrive on Time	30
Arriving Late For an Interview	31
Respect the Interviewer's Time	31

The Job Interview Volume 2

Dress Appropriately   32
   Understand the Organization's Attire Standards   34
   Appropriate Attire   34
   Inappropriate Attire   36
   Wrinkled, Frayed and Dirty Clothing   37
Aroma Therapy   37
   Drinking Coffee or Smoking Prior to the Interview   38
   Will Your Smoke Breaks Hamper Productivity   38
   Can Smoking Eliminate You From Consideration
   Will Your Perfume or Cologne Offend the Interviewer   39
   Will Your Fragrance Remind the Interviewer of Someone   40
   Hygiene & Grooming   41
   Shower   41
   Shave   41
Sit, Relax, Stay a While   42
   Take All Appointments Off of Your Calendar   42
   Be Prepared to Pay One Hour Parking Fees   43
   Plan Your Route   43
Negative Statements   44
   Could Negativity Eliminate You From Consideration   44
   Ask Yourself did your statements send the following messages   45
      You Do Not Take Accountability for Your Actions or Errors   45
      You May Not Work Well With Others   46
      You May Have Contempt for Authority   47
      You May Become a Negative Influence in the Workplace   48
Poor Work History   49
   Are there Serious Issues With Your Behavior   50
   Are You Able to Perform Your Assigned Duties   50
Poor Credit History   51

　　　　Will You Embezzle Organization Funds　52
　　　　Criminal History　53
　　　　Be Honest　55
　　　　Slang and Jargon　55

PART IV
THE INTERVIEW　57
　　Group Interviews　57
　　Behavioral and Situational Interviews　58
　　Skype Interviews　59
　　Every Question Could Have a Hidden Meaning　60
　　　　Why Interviewers use Complicated Questions　61
　　Hidden Meanings Behind Interview Questions　62
　　Illegal Question　65
　　　　Why Personal Questions are Illegal　65
　　　　Sample Illegal Questions　65
　　Sample Interview Questions　66
　　The Information Age　69
　　A Few interview Do's and Don'ts　70
　　Handshake　71
　　Greet the Interviewer　71
　　Turn off Your Cellular Phone　71
　　Bring an extra Copy of Your Resume　72
　　Make Eye Contact　72
　　Good Questions to Ask an Interviewer　74
　　Being asked to Multiple Interviews　75

PART V
APPENDIX: ADDITIONAL INFORMATION
EMPLOYMENT RESOURCES
　　Employment Security Commissions
　　　　http://www.job-hunt.org/index.html
　　Federal Job Websites
　　　　Fedworld.com
　　　　Federalgovernmentjobs.us/search
　　Government Job Web Sites
　　　　USAjobs.opm.gov
　　Military Job Web Sites

Health Care Job Websites
- Healthcareweb.com
- Medzilla.com
- Healthcarejobsite.com
- MiracleWorkers.com/Medical_Jobs

Corporate Job Search
- Career Builders
- Monster.com
- College grad.com
- HBCU Connect.com
- Simplyhired.com
- CollegeRecruiter.com
- Hotjobs.com
- JobFoc.com
- Indeed.com
- Jobing.com
- BilingualCareer.com
- CareerPark.com
- Dice.com
- Snagajob.com
- http://www.job-hunt.org/state_unemployment_offices.shtml
- http://www.quintcareers.com/top_50_sites.html
- http://www.quintcareers.com/general_resources.htm

State Government Sites

State Employment Sites

References

Special Thanks

Lamont Jackson

Introduction

This book is intended to assist people seeking employment. It is not an "end all" for this topic nor is it intended to be a "rule and guide" for interviewing. This book was written to provide a brief, to the point explanation of the interview process. It was also written to provide tools, which an applicant could use, to enhance his or her interviewing capabilities. The information presented may be general knowledge to some. In other instances, this book may present information which is entirely new to you. In either situation, if you are seeking employment then this book was written to add perspective to the actual process of the interview and some of its purposes. "The Job Interview" shares the employer's perspective as it applies to the actual job interview.

As a rule, during my workshops, I always stress the importance of being honest during the interview process. Failing to do so could result in adverse conditions during the interview or after you're employed.

PART I

An Invitation to Interview

An invitation to a job interview says a lot about your education, training, experience and abilities. If you were invited to an interview, you should congratulate yourself. There is good news in the invitation. The good news could mean your application or resume has caught the attention of someone in the human resources department. It could also mean your education or work experience is impressive and deserves further consideration. In all, if you were invited to an interview it meant you met the minimum qualifications for the position. However, being asked to an interview is just the first step in what could be a series of interviews. Remember, an invitation to interview rarely means the interview process is just a formality. Nor does an invitation to interview mean you will be hired immediately.

Being able to present yourself positively is extremely important. I once heard a colleague say "College along with an application and a well written resume will only get an individual in the front door". My colleague went on to say "Once the applicant is inside, they still have to convince me that they are the right person for the position". My colleague's all believed when interviewing applicants with similar qualifications and experience, the final decision could favor the applicant with the strongest interview skills.

For most of us, the interview process can be extremely stressful. The point of a person or persons sitting across the table from us holds a key to the gate of employment, could cause us to become a nervous wreck. A little known secret is these gatekeepers are often as nervous as the person that they are interviewing. The person selected by an HR department or an interviewer says a lot about their ability to critically review their applicants. Selecting unqualified applicants could negatively impact their careers. Likewise, selecting applicants with sketchy backgrounds or unfavorable character traits could have like results.

There are many factors involved when selecting a person for employment. Some of the obvious factors for an applicant's consideration include:
- Education
- Experience
- Professionalism
- Position specific training
- Skills you have which are applicable to the specific job being offered
- Your ability to fit into an established system

However, there are also other areas the interviewer is trying to uncover. Education, career goals, experience and training can be a vital part of the selection process. However, the interviewer is also interested in the applicant's background and character traits. They will want to understand and expose any area which could:
- Hamper production
- Cause conflict among the existing staff
- Expose the organization to costly litigation

Employers will not hire a candidate if they believe the applicant will hamper productivity in any manner. This is especially true when the revenue stream involves a significant amount of teamwork. If the employers are unable to bring their products and services to the marketplace, there could be a significant decline in revenue. Likewise, if a newly hired employee brings their counterproductive habits into a collaborative environment, it could have an adverse effect on the organizations revenues. Their destructive point of view could slowly break down the fibers of cohesiveness which an organization needs to function at an optimal level.

Employers must monitor the entire organization and are observing every variable, which increases or decreases the organizations productivity and revenues. When there is a decline in productivity or revenues, the employer's livelihood depends on their ability to identify the origin of the decline, and make the necessary adjustments quickly. Their failure to recognize and make adjustments as soon as possible could have disastrous consequences for their organization. Therefore, the employee variable in the productivity equation is a significant component in the success or ultimate failure of an organization.

Although employers are concerned with their organizations productivity, and the candidate's ability to fit into an established system, the law forbids them from disqualifying a candidate based on the following:

- Race
- Height & Weight
- Credit Rating Or Economic Status
- Religious Affiliation Or Beliefs
- Citizenship
- Marital Status, Number Of Children
- Gender
- Arrest & Conviction
- Security/Background Checks For Certain Religious Or Ethnic Groups
- Disability
- Medical Questions & Examinations

The U.S. Equal Employment Opportunity Commission's lists the following information, on its website, with regard to discrimination in the workplace:
The U.S. Equal Employment Opportunity Commission (EEOC) enforces Federal laws which prohibit discrimination in

Lamont Jackson

the workplace. The law the Equal Employment Opportunity Commission enforces laws which forbid discrimination in every aspect of employment. The laws enforced by EEOC prohibit an employer or other covered entity from using neutral employment policies and practices that have a disproportionately negative effect on applicants or employees of a particular race, color, religion, sex (including pregnancy), or national origin, or on an individual with a disability or class of individuals with disabilities, if the polices or practices at issue are not job-related and necessary to the operation of the business.

It is also illegal for an employer to recruit new employees in a way that discriminates against them because of their race, color, religion, sex (including pregnancy), national origin, age (40 or older), disability or genetic information. (Page 1)

If you believe you are the victim of discrimination, because of your race, color, religion, sex (including pregnancy), national origin, age (40 or older), disability or genetic information, you can file a **Complaint of Discrimination** with The U.S. Equal Employment Opportunity Commission.

The EEOC can be contacted on their website at **http://www.eeoc.gov/contact/**.

A process of elimination

As an employer I have interviewed candidates for multiple positions. A majority of my workforce have been wonderful employees. They were easily introduced into the workforce, able to learn our system and had a positive impact on production. Unfortunately, while most of my newly hired staff became ideal employees, there were some which were not the right fit for my organization. These undesirable employees were often disruptive, negligent, held contempt for authority, slowed production and were highly confrontational. These employees were presented well, on paper and always interviewed very well. Unfortunately, their behavior and performance was, universally, far below an acceptable level.

There may never be a truly fail proof method of selecting a candidates for any position. However, properly reviewing an applicant's education, employment history and background lessens an organization's likelihood of hiring an unacceptable employee. The interview process is an indispensable resource for employers. The interview process is one way companies can review applicants based on a specific set of requirements whereby the best fit can usually be selected.

An organization's hiring requirements are usually established to:
- Assess an applicant's ability to perform the job functions
- Evaluate an applicant's experience and work history
- Limit the interviewer to a set of prerequisites which would decrease and or eliminate bias against any applicant

In my experience, most candidates' were eliminated based on their words and actions during the initial minutes of the interview. In most cases, the candidate arrived more than 10 minutes late, had falsified information on their application, gave answers that was different from the information on their resume or application, or exhibited behaviors which were clearly unacceptable. Once a candidate arrived for a second interview and was dress inappropriately. The candidate's attire offended my colleague and the candidate was not interviewed. Later, the same day, my colleague and I discussed the candidate. When I ask my colleague opinion of the matter, my colleague replied. "The candidate's attire was intended to provide them an unfair advantage in this interview and I am offended by the candidate's actions". I was in full agreement and we moved on to the next candidate and later filled the position.

When an employer posts a position they could receive more than 2 dozen applications. The HR department may have a short amount of time to select a specific number of applicants to interview. In some situations, the HR department may be given only a set number of available interview slots. I have routinely instructed my staff to present the 5 most qualified applicants and from them I may only interview 3 or 4. Therefore, if my staff is looking at a stack of 25 applications or resumes, they will review and immediately separate the unqualified applicants first. The most qualified applicants from the remaining stack will be reviewed again. At this point, the remaining applications could have dropped from 25 to 18. Next, my staff will give the education, training and work experience a closer look. This could lower the stack of applications down to 8 or 10. Once the most qualified applicants are identified, interviews are set and the question and answer process begins.

Why companies are so selective

If you ever wondered why the interview process is so meticulous, or why you were asked to interview, for a position, more than once, I will provide the following scenario. Consider this, if you were planning to hire someone to repair your vehicle, how you would judge the mechanic? Would you want to take your vehicle to a certified shop or would you want to save a few dollars and ask your neighbor to complete the job? If you considered both options, you could imagine the up and down side for both. If you used an uncertified mechanic, you may save a few dollars. Yet there could be problems later, and the uncertified mechanic could recharge you for those future repairs. Some of which may have been caused by their negligence. Using a certified mechanic may cost a little more but, the work is usually guaranteed and the mechanic has received the most up to date training.

If you were going out for dinner and needed a sitter for your child or your pet, would you take a chance on an unknown person with a sketchy background or, would you hire a person you knew or trusted? If you considered the high probability of problems associated with an unknown or uncertified person, then you are thinking like an employer.

However, if you are not viewing this information like an employer, you may only see the negative aspects of the interview. If you would prefer to have your home, your child or even your pet in the care of an unproven or unknown person to save a few dollars then you may well get what you paid for. Additionally, in most cases, the benefits, associated with saving a few dollars, rarely outweigh the potential losses.

As an employer, I assess the applicants on the job requirement, their qualifications for the job and how well the candidate will fit into my organization and become a productive employee. As I wrote earlier, employers are prohibited from discriminating against a person based on their race, age, religion by law. Therefore, an applicant's abilities and qualifications should be the primary factor in an employer's decision process. Other factors may be used, but the areas listed on the Department of Labor's website should not be.

PART II

Preparing for the Interview

When I interviewed candidates I am always amazed by their lack of preparedness. I estimate that only 4 out of every 10 candidates knew some basic information about my organization. At any time a person could log onto a home computer or a computer at a public library, and gather a fair amount of data on my organization. Likewise, information about an organization you are interested in could be found by doing a simple Google search.

As an employer, I am very interested in applicants with some knowledge of my organization. Also, I am interested in individuals which have some knowledge of my industry. As the old saying goes, "the more you know the more you grow". If a person applies for a position with my organization, I am less likely to hire someone that has absolutely no idea what my organization does. If they have no knowledge of what we do, how could they make a meaningful contribution to my organization? I would be concerned that they are only applying for a position and would be with my organization until another position becomes available.

I suggest bringing information about your work with you to an interview. While it is not recommended that you display it during the interview, I do recommend that you have it with you, so that you could review your information prior to the start of the interview. Having a sheet of paper with your work history can be a good reference. I have asked candidates about previous work experience, and they were eliminated from consideration because they were unable to clearly express the duties they performed. I find it acceptable for a person to have a few notes that they could refer to about past work experience. Experience is the key when it comes to finding employment.

The Resume

Not all employers require a resume for every posted position. Generally, when a resume is not required, employers make determinations based on the information listed on an application. More often than not, the job posting will let you know if a resume is required or not.

In a nutshell, a resume is an excellent method of summarizing your employment history and experience, along with your education, relevant technical, administrative and other skills.

I usually shy away from discussions regarding resumes. This is an area that I am not fond of. As an employer, I am more interested in the content within an applicant's resume than its format. I look for qualification, skills and abilities. While it is important to have a resume that is properly formatted, I rarely eliminate applicants from consideration for having a poorly formatted resume.

Generally, I am far less concerned with a resumes layout, than I am with the content it contains. I have reviewed many resumes that were perfectly formatted, yet they lacked substance or relevance to an open position. With this said, I must admit that I spoke with 10 colleagues about this issue, and I received 10 different opinions regarding a resumes format.

One person stated that they would not consider a resume if it was more than one page. Another stated that if there were more than 4 bullet points, for each position held, they would set the resume aside. One colleague preferred having the education section listed first, while another would only consider resumes that displayed the work history first and the skills and experiences listed last.

I generally offer a simple suggestion. If you do not have a resume, consider contacting a person that could help you with this. If you have a resume but are not sure if it is professional enough for the position for which you are applying, I suggest that you speak with someone that could help you with improvements. If you are familiar with anyone working in the human resources field, I would say asking them for help would defiantly be a step in the right direction.

If you are not associated with anyone in the human resources field, or are unable to establish a relationship with someone with resume writing experience, I would suggest following a format that is fairly consistent. There are a least four topics that should be on your resume. They are:

1. Your Contact information, which includes the following:

    a. Your personal email address
    b. Your home address
    c. An accurate phone number

2. Relevant work experience
3. Abilities/skills
4. Education

In my experience, I find that the opinions on a resumes format are so varied, that it is sometimes difficult or nearly impossible to create one that would be free from some sort of critical analysis. Just remember, every person has a different view and no two views are alike. Find a format that is suitable and professional and begin there. This could allow you to edit and adjust your resume as you see fit.

Lamont Jackson

Accurate Contact Information

Accurate contact information is extremely important. The contact information you provide may be the only available information an employer has when they are interested in contacting you. Therefore, if your contact information is inaccurate, an employer might set your application aside causing you to miss a potential employment opportunity.

Similarly, your application could be tossed in the trash or placed into a non-active status file. To avoid missing out on possible employment offers, always ensure your contact information is accurate. Even if your address or phone number changes, it is always a good idea to update all information with any company that you have filed an application with.

As I stated earlier, when a position becomes available, my staff select's the most qualified applicants. After which they narrow the group to around ten. The selected applicants are contacted and interviews are then scheduled. However, when my staff attempts to contact an applicant, and the information is inaccurate, they are removed from consideration.

Over the years there have been a number of highly qualified applicants that failed to provide accurate contact information. As an employer, I find it extremely frustrating when I attempt to reach out to an applicant, and their contact information is not accurate. Without accurate contact information, how could an employer invite you to an interview?

Are your Phone Numbers Active

It may seem odd to some that individuals should be reminded to provide accurate contact information. As an employer, my staff and I have reviewed and were impressed by many well qualified applicants. Unfortunately, we were also amazed that a number of those applicants failed to provide a means to be contacted.

On numerous occasions, a member of my staff, attempted to contact applicants and discovered that their contact information was inaccurate. Many of these applicants would then, contact my office to inquire about their application status. After my staff explains why we were unable to contact them, the applicant's replies are oddly similar. Someone in your office must have changed the number, I may have written the number wrong, or my favorite, you must be looking at the wrong phone number. I will say each of these excuses says a lot about the applicant.

- If the number was written incorrectly, what is the likelihood of that applicant incorrectly filling out an organization document? If the document is sent to a client or stakeholder what would it say about my organization?
- Someone in my office changed the number. This would lead me to believe the applicant is not accountable. Also, this is a bit offensive as it implies my organization is in the business of preferential hiring or tampers with documents. But in all it leads me to believe the applicant will be a counterproductive employee.
- I may be looking at the wrong number. This is the most offensive of all excuses I have heard. It implies the person reviewing the application is incompetent.

Here is some food for thought. If you are informed that your contact information is incorrect, simply provide the correct information. Do not become combative, intimidating or issue unfounded accusations. These reactions rarely yield positive results.

Voice Mail

I am sure that you have placed a call to someone in the past, and was held hostage by their voice mail music that lasted 3 minutes long. I would guess the same could be said about lengthy voice messages that caused you to end the call immediately. Employers rarely interview a single applicant for a job opening. In many situations, multiple applicants are selected for an interview. With this in mind it is important to note that the longer your voice message, the shorter the call will be. If I place a call to a potential applicant and I hear a long or unnecessary voice message, or there is music that plays for longer than a few seconds, usually, I will hang up and move on to the next applicant.

If you are an applicant and you're waiting for a call from a Human Resources Department, I suggest that you record a brief voice mail message. Generally, a simple voice mail message would be adequate. I would suggest that your refrain from messages with an aggressive tone, or that displays a lack of concern.

Lengthy voice mails could cause you to miss a job announcement. If an employer must listen to your rendition of the latest popular song, the call could end and your chance of employment would end along with it. A suggested voice mail message could be along the following lines:
- "Thank you for calling, I'm sorry I missed your call, I will return your call shortly".

- "Thank you for calling, this is (your name), I am on another call but I will contact you as soon as possible"
- "This is (your name), I'm sorry I missed your call, please leave a message and I will contact you as soon as possible".

If you have not recorded a voice mail message, it may be a good idea to do so prior to placing your number on an application. As you are recording your voice mail message consider two things.

- Who might hear your message
- Will your voice mail message offend someone

Create a Better Email Account

Your e-mail address is another crucial piece of information. An employer could imply more from your e-mail address than necessary. This is especially true if an employer has a pet peeve for unprofessional e-mail addresses. If an employer had such a disposition, it could cause you to be eliminated from consideration for employment. I have seen some very interesting email addresses. Many of the email addresses that I have seen on applications have range from being inappropriately sexual to downright disgusting. As an employer, I would be concerned about a person with an email address like:
- foolofthemonth@whateveryouremaicompany.com
- hotone@whateveryouremailcompany.com
- Thethickestone@blank.com

I suggest that you create a professional e-mail address for future applications. If you have not created a professional email account, please do so as soon as possible. There are a number of sites which offer free email addresses, so creating an email address that is used solely for professional purposes would not put a strain on your personal finances.

Here are a few suggestions for a professional email address:
- Your first initial and last name @ *whateveryouremailcompany.com*.
- jsmit@whateveryouremailcompany.com.com
- johnsmith@whateveryouremailcompany.com
- john.smith@whateveryouremailcompany.com
- smithj@whateveryouremailcompany.com
- smithjohn@whateveryouremailcompany.com

The examples listed are just a few of many options available to you. In some situations your first and last names may not be available. If your name is not available, or if you are not comfortable using your name as part of your email, my suggestion would be to build an email account that is as professional as possible.

Note: whateveryouremailcompany.com may or may not be an actual organization. Any similarities to this name or any email names listed whatsoever are purely coincidental.

Know the organization

I am always amazed by how little applicants knew about my organization when they applied. I interviewed many applicants that would ask, "What do you guys do here". As an employer, I could not justify hiring a person that does not at least know the basic information about my organization. When you apply for a position, it is a good idea to have some knowledge about the organization and its products and services. It may not be necessary to study every aspect of an organization. However, if an applicant is applying with my organization, I would believe they should at least know a little about what we do. Not knowing what we do would lead me to believe the applicant would take off as soon as the next best thing comes along.

Being knowledgeable of the organization and its products and services could lead to additional consideration from the interviewer. Here are a few research suggestions.

What do you really know about a potential employer?

Prior to the interview, it may be a good idea to do a little research. When researching a future employer, I suggest that you have a basic understanding of a potential employer's products or services. A point to remember, you will not need a file the size of a library reference book. However, any information you obtain could be beneficial.

Research the interviewer

If you are able to obtain the name of the interviewer, I suggest a basic review of his or her LinkedIn page. Many human resource professionals are on LinkedIn. Having some basic knowledge from their page could assist you in establishing a rapport with the interviewer.

Here are a few research possibilities:
    I. What are interests
    II. What schools did they attend
    III. What are their hobbies
    IV. What organizations are they a member of

Just be mindful that LinkedIn users are able to see the individuals that have viewed their page. So if you choose to review their page, it might be a good idea to be prepared to discuss your intent for viewing their page.

Here are a few additional research possibilities:

    I. What products or services does the employer provide
    II. Is the organization a local company with a few employees or an organization with hundreds or even thousands of employees
    III. How well is the company performing
    IV. Information about the company's competitors

- **Products or services offered**

    I. Understand if the organization sells round widgets of square pegs
    II. Understand who uses the company products (men, women, children, pets etc.)
    III. New products, recently introduced to the market, by the company

- **Amount of products sold per year**

    I. Not always necessary, however, if you are applying for a position in sales, marketing, or management, it could be something worth knowing

- **Latest products or services introduced and how well the organization is performing in the market**

    I. Not always necessary, however, if you are applying for a position in sales, marketing, or management, it could be something worth knowing

Understanding the organization's products and finances could open a dialogue for new product development, marketing suggestions and forecasting trends. An unknown opportunity could present itself during the interview. Having additional knowledge of an organization's products, services, and even finances could show that you are thinking forward and may be an asset to the organization. This could be the difference between you receiving an offer for employment.

When was the organization established?

This may not apply in every situation; however, if you are applying for a position in sales, marketing, or management, it could be something worth knowing. Some clients and investors may be drawn to companies that have been in business for more than a few years. Companies that have been in business for a while may have a stronger background. The stronger background could result in stronger organizational policies and procedures, as well as a stronger organizational structure.

Lamont Jackson

Any changes in board members or executive staff positions

Having knowledge of executive of governing board changes might not apply in every situation; however, if it does, changes in these positions or appointments could be a very important piece of information. This is especially relevant if the new executive team was hired to make changes within the organization.

It could be helpful if you understood the reason for any changes at the executive level. When researching an organization, it might be helpful to know if the changes within the executive staff were made due to financial troubles within the organization. Another thought to consider might be, could the new administration have an interest in realigning or eliminating certain positions within the organization?

The new executive team might be planning a few duty realignments, or could be planning to eliminate certain positions. Streamlining the duties of their staff might be planned to lower the organizations expenses.

Additionally, the executive team might be ready to eliminate employees or positions that have become ineffective. Changes within the executive team may have been caused by the current management team's inability or unwillingness to make the necessary adjustments whereby production and profits were hindered.

Additionally, changes in the Executive staff could signal that the organization has become frustrated with its current management team or in the direction that the team has taken the organization.

The newly hired executives might be ready to make sweeping changes within the organization. Having some knowledge of the organizations issues, along with a few well-crafted suggestions could lead to additional consideration from the interviewer.

Here are a few research suggestions:

- **Where the organization was founded (in which country, state or city)**
    - Not always necessary, however, if you are applying for a position in sales, marketing, or management, it could be something worth knowing
- **Any location changes in the past few years**
    - Not always necessary, however, if you are applying for a position in sales, marketing, or management, it could be something worth knowing
- **Number of employees**
    - This would give you an idea of the labor force you will be working with or may eventually manage
- **Number of executives**
    - This could be helpful if you are seeking an executive position
- **Number of Board members**
    - This could be helpful if you are seeking an executive position
- **Number of Middle and Lower level managers**
    - This could be helpful if you are seeking an executive position
- **Administrative staff size**
    - This would give you an idea of the labor force you will be working with or may eventually manage
- **Number of departments**

- This would give you an idea of the labor force you will be working with or may eventually manage
- **Department Functions**
  - This would give you an idea of the labor force you will be working with or may eventually manage

Financial Information (Annual Report)

Being knowledgeable of the organization's financial standing could also lead to additional consideration from the interviewer. This information could be used by applicants seeking executive level positions. Understanding basic financial information could assist you in determining how well the organization is being managed. Additionally, understanding the organization's finances could tell you if this organization is the right fit for your career.

Most organizations have a staff person dedicated to external communications. This person could assist you in gathering the research information you need. Place a call to the organization, ask to be connected with the designated employee, and explain why the information is being requested. If all else fails, the organizations website has most of the non-confidential information that you would need

Here are two research suggestions:

- **An Organization's Annual Report** – This provides a summary of the how well or poorly an organization performed during the year
- **The Organization Chart**- This chart illustrates the structure of the organization. A review of this chart will help you understand the number of departments

an organization has and how the departments interact. Lastly, the Organization Chart will show which person heads which department, how the department's report to one another.

Is the organization is unionized

Some companies may have a stellar relationship with the local union. However, some companies may have long standing issues with its collective bargaining agreement and could be looking for person to assist them in working through their differences. In either situation, having some familiarity in this area could be beneficial, if your input is requested.

How many members

It could be helpful to know the size of an organization's workforce. In most cases, newly hired employees are absorbed into the union once their probationary period ends. Understanding the organizations workforce makeup and its size is always helpful.

Local Union Name

The type of union is easily understood based on its name in most cases. Also, if you are unable to gather information on the organization or its operation, knowing the type of union or the name of the union they held a bargaining agreement with could be helpful as well. If the organization has a local pipe fitters union or an electrical union local 1011, for example, you may reasonably assume the organization manufactures, sells or are in the construction, plumbing or electrical industry.

Union's information, its leadership and policies and the organizations relationship with the union

This topic should have a full chapter dedicated to the pros and cons of a collective bargaining agreement. For the purpose of this book, I will maintain a brief overview and offer more information later.

The organizations executive staffs could have issues with parts of the collective bargaining agreement. Likewise, the union's leadership might have issues of their own with the organization, or parts of the collective bargaining agreement. This information could be helpful if you are an employee which may be absorbed into the union once your probationary period expires. This could mean, you are required to pay a certain amount of money monthly in dues once you are placed into the union. The amounts could be as low as $1 or more than $100 per month.

If you are a manager or future department head, it would help to understand the environment you may be walking into and how you could assist in creating a better environment. Then again, identifying these issues could tell you if the job is the right fit for you.

Know the Salary
Salary Range

If an organization posts a position and the salary is not listed, it would be a good idea to have some knowledge of current pay rates for the field you are entering. An organization may have an annual budget of $35K for an administrative assistant. An employer will ask your salary requirements. If you are unaware of the competitive salaries for your field and your reply is $25K you have potentially undersold yourself by $10K.

Likewise, if a position is budgeted for $35K and you DEMAND 40K, an organization may pass on you, even if you are a stronger candidate than someone willing to work for less. Also, some companies may be able to justify paying $5K over their budgeted amounts if you are an exceptional candidate. In either case, it is important to know the position, the salary for the position and the salary range for individuals in the same field. Also, researching the organization and understanding the organizations, financial standings could help you when negotiating your salary.

When you are asked a question about your salary expectations, I have found one of the most acceptable responses was when candidate's stated their current salary, followed by expressing their ideal salary as being near or slightly above their current salary. I made an offer of employment to a candidate and during salary negotiations the candidate replied, "I earn $27K and would be interested in a salary close to that amount". I found this interesting, because the position paid $33K which meant I could have hired the candidate and remained within my budget. Also, I had a bit of wiggle room to work with if needed.

Understanding the salary requirements of a position cannot be overstated. If you are changing fields or are unsure of your salary requirements, there are websites dedicated to assisting applicants with salary ranges for a given position. Websites like mysalary.com, Salary.com and Payscale.com allows you to research salary ranges by industry. It is important to understand that these are salary ranges and should be weighed against your understanding of the local economy along with any other information about the organization, and its financial standing.

A final note about salary expectations, researching sites like Payscale.com, mysalary.com and salary.com provides industry specific information about various industries. This information could be weighed heavily when you are preparing to negotiate your salary. Remember, negotiations require two or more persons. With this in mind, it is important to understand the need for you to be flexible during negotiations.

Know the position

Another area that I noticed similar deficiencies was the applicant's knowledge of the position they are applying for. Whenever I ask candidates what they knew about the position they applied for, they were uniformly baffled by the question. Most would say, "not much' they follow-up with a hollow answer bout the position. If you were applying for a position as a chef, I think knowledge of recipes, restaurant and kitchen operational methods and prompt, quality service would be commonly known.

Likewise, as a truck driver, you may not know how a restaurant runs or how to organize a staff of 5 cooks but you would know how to fill out a log book and how to adjust your truck axels. Similarly, you would understand how the weigh stations, located on every interstate, operate. Therefore, it is important to understand and be able to express your understanding of the position you are applying for. If you are unable to do so, do not be ashamed to go out and research the position.

Once, I hired a person with limited experience and the employee worked out well in the beginning. However, the employee's conduct quickly deteriorated once the probationary period ended. When I spoke with the employee about his conduct, the employee said, I really didn't understand what I was getting into when I took this job. It is becoming more than I expected and I can't keep up. Fortunately this was identified early and I was able to retrain and provide more strategies for the employee whereby his job was easier to manage.

Social Media

Libraries are good place to research an organization. However, I suggest logging onto the internet and performing a basic site search for company information. Visiting a company's web site can be very helpful. Information about a company's products, services, financial information and more can be found on a company's website. Reviewing the information listed on a company's website could provide most of the information that you would need for an interview.

Social media can be an excellent source of information about a potential Employer. Sites like Facebook and LinkedIn allows employers, like myself, an opportunity to create a company page.

Viewing company information on Facebook helps you to understand the company and gather some basic information. Each company has a photo page, and viewing that page could provide some understanding of a company's culture. Some company's posts photos of their staff, recent or past events, and their work sites. Also a company can list updates on Facebook on a regular basis. This allows viewers to see recent changes or updates to their products and services.

Like Facebook, LinkedIn currently has a very strong presence on the internet. LinkedIn's company pages allow employers to post comprehensive information about their products and services as well. However, LinkedIn is like a mini website for a company. A company can list the most of the information that it has on its website, but in smaller amounts. Also, one feature that I find most impressive about LinkedIn is the Careers and insights pages. Individuals can review the company's hiring philosophy, view video posts, review lists of companies with similar products or services, and the pages of their executives and employees. All of which could improve your understanding of the company.

Employees can create a page on LinkedIn and when they open their individual pages, they will see recommendations for linking their page to other employees within the company. Therefore, when you open a company's LinkedIn page, you could view the pages of their employees and view their profiles. By viewing employee pages you could gain a better understanding of the types of individuals employed by the company, and their interests or philosophy's.

PART III

The Interview Process

Arrive on time

Arriving late for a scheduled interview can be one of the brightest red flags an applicant could raise. There is nothing more frustrating than having a block of time set aside for interviews and the applicant arrives late. I have few spare hours in a given day. When a candidate is identified, I usually set aside one hour for their interview. Therefore, when an applicant arrives after a scheduled time, I will instruct my staff to send them away. Generally, if a candidate cannot arrive on time for an interview, I understand this to be an early performance indicator.

I usually maintain a minimum of six applications for a given position. If a candidate cannot arrive on time, I will move on to the next candidate. If an applicant knows they are running behind schedule, I will postpone an interview if they called my office and explained their situation. However, if a call is not made, the applicant is turned around as soon as they arrive.

An applicant that arrives late for a scheduled interview can send two distinct messages.

1. They may have an issue arriving, on time, for an assigned shift
2. They may have poor work and scheduling habits.

If you are unable to arrive for an assigned shift it may cause a co-worker to work extra hours to cover for you. Additionally, this would increase an organization's overtime hours.

Poor work habits could mean you may be unable to remain on task throughout the day. This could also mean you are unable to multi-task or prioritize tasks. These issues could hamper productivity resulting in decreased revenues for an organization.

Arriving late for an interview

I will address this topic in plain terms, NEVER, NEVER, NEVER, miss a scheduled interview!!! If an employer or Human Resources Employee schedules you for an interview, you have positively presented yourself and are qualified for a position. This means you have met the minimum qualifications, and require further screening. As I wrote in the introduction, being asked to an interview rarely means the interview is a formality and you will be hired immediately. Usually, further employment and background screenings are needed. Therefore, it is important to arrive on time, a few minutes early if possible, and prepared to stay as long as necessary.

It is never a positive sign when a candidate arrives after a scheduled time. Most open positions draw multiple applications. Once an application is received and reviewed, the most qualified applicants, based on a set of position requirements are invited to an interview. Arriving after a schedule appointment could eliminate you from consideration.

Respect the interviewer's time

Most human resources professionals are extremely busy people. When they schedule a meeting or interview with a candidate, it is in the candidate's best interest to arrive on time. Failing to arrive on time for a schedule interview rarely interpreted positively. Often, it could be a major warning sign to the employer. If the employer believes that your tardiness was an indication of future issues, then it could cause you to be eliminated from consideration.

As an applicant, consider the employer take on late arrivals. A few thoughts that an employer may conclude from your tardiness could be:

- You could be a person that habitually arrives late for assigned shifts.
- You are not organized
- You may be a person that is unable to remain on task
- You may be a person that is unable to complete projects in a timely manner.

If you are granted an interview, I suggest that you plan to arrive at least 10 minutes early. Arriving early allows you enough time to compose yourself and review your resume. Arriving early also allows you time to assess the organizations environment along with an apparent signs of its operating culture.

Dress appropriately

Dressing appropriately should be two words which require little explanation. However, More often than not, I have interviewed candidates and they wore clothes more suited for an evening at the local club than for an office environment. In many instances, candidates clothing was less than ideal for a work environment.

Candidates should understand the interview begins long before the first words are spoken. The interview begins before they enter the interviewer's office. To better explain this, let's use an example from chapter 1. If you were planning to hire someone to repair your vehicle, how would judge the mechanic if you arrived and the mechanics shop was kept in order and he or she was wearing coveralls or some sort of uniform, would you give them a positive first assessment? Likewise, if the shop had only a few cars on its lot waiting for repairs, yet they seem to have been there for less than a week, would you feel comfortable leaving your car with this mechanic?

On the other hand, let's say the mechanics shop was untidy, and there were parts scattered around the shop, which seems out dated and have been there for an extended period, would you feel comfortable with that mechanic? Let's say there were many cars in the lot, which seemed abandoned or the lot looked more like a junk yard than a repair shop, would you feel comfortable?

This is something we consider when servicing our personal vehicles. If you go to a mechanic and the job is performed poorly, you end up paying for the same job twice. Additionally, when the job is performed, yet they use substandard parts or parts which should place on a manufactures recall list to save a few dollars, your safety is then in jeopardy every time you drive your vehicle.

An employer's initial observation could lessen a candidate employment opportunity, when the candidate fails to dress appropriately. Candidates that arrive for an interview inappropriately dressed could lead an employer to believe the candidate has limits in their attention to detail. Also, an employer could view this as a candidate's unwillingness or inability to adjust to changing organization standards. Simply put, by dressing appropriately, candidate's project confidence, appear more organized, shows they understand interviewing decorum and are ready to present themselves as an ambassador of the organization.

Understand the organization's attire standards

If you have been in the workforce for any length of time, then you should have a reasonable understanding of organizations attire standards. What works for one industry will not necessarily work for another. Most Information Technology (or I.T.) guys that I know are accustomed to wearing golf shirts to work. On the other hand, many of the computer programmers that I know will come to work in whatever they pulled out of the laundry bin that morning. I often laugh at how both have similar fields but have completely different dress standards.

As a candidate for a position, consider the following:

- **Is casual clothing acceptable**
- **If it is, what is the organizations definition of casual?**
- **Are ties, pant suits, calf length dresses the established and acceptable attire?**
- **If not, what is appropriate work attire?**

Appropriate Attire

As an applicant it is important to remember, your first impression could have a lasting effect on the entire interview. Understanding the organization and its mission could be helpful when considering your clothing options. The following information may be helpful as you prepare for your interview.

Men

Men should consider wearing a suit, especially when interviewing for positions within the administrative, executive, managerial and certain operational fields.

- Navy blue or charcoal gray business suits are usually acceptable
- A white shirt along and a tie with conservative tie pattern are always wise choices
- Clean, well-polished black shoes (with laces) are a good option

For men that prefer facial hair, it is always a good idea to have beards and mustaches short and neatly trimmed for an interview. Also, it would be a good idea to remove all piercing's and cover any tattoos is much as possible. This is especially valid if you are interviewing for an administrative, executive, managerial or certain operational positions.

Women

Most employers I spoke with stated a two piece business suit or a long-sleeved blouse are ideal when interviewing for positions within the administrative, executive, managerial and certain operational fields.

- Limit earrings to one pair when interviewing
- Stockings that resembles your natural skin tone could be a wise option

If you prefer high heeled shoes it may be a good idea to wear a medium length heel. Additionally, clear fingernail polish or a conservative color is also wise options. Also, it would be a good idea to remove all piercing's and cover any tattoos is much as possible. Lastly, necklaces, chains, pearls and other forms of jewelry should be limited and not very large.

Inappropriate Attire

I would assume this topic needs no explanation. However, I have interviewed candidates who have treaded across the line of appropriateness. If you are not sure about your attire for an interview, please consider this. If you are wearing any item which would offend or make someone uncomfortable, then another clothing option may be required. If your personal views are on any item, clothing hats, briefcase, etc., you may want to consider another option. If your clothing offers an opinion which may be openly disputed during the interview, you may want to consider another clothing option. Lastly, if your attire is deemed inappropriate, the interviewer may become biased against you. This could negatively affect the outcome of your interview.

There are a few images and messages you may want to avoid when you are assembling your attire for an interview. These images and messages include:

- Clothing with nudity or obscene messages
- Racially insensitive images or messages
- Religious images or messages
- Political images or messages
- Profane images or messages
- Other images or messages which could be conceived as insensitive or offensive
- Any clothing which could be viewed as unprofessional
- Any clothing which would cause you to be un-presentable as an agent of the organization
- Profane or inappropriate tattoos

Lamont Jackson

Wrinkled, Frayed and Dirty Clothing

If you do not have an iron, consider borrowing one. Remember you are applying for a position and if selected, you would be an ambassador for the organization. Therefore it is important to dedicate a few extra minutes towards your appearance. When you arrive for an interview wearing wrinkled clothing or clothing that's dirty or frayed, the interviewer may assume the following:

- You are unmotivated
- You are not truly interested in the position
- You may not pay attention to details
- You are not organized

Again, you may want to avoid anything that could eliminate you from consideration for employment.

Aroma Therapy

In 1997 my wife and I applied for a job at a hospital in Georgia. Interestingly enough, the first question we were asked was "do you smoke?" We were asked that question before we were given an application. Neither my wife nor I were smokers. I thought that was an odd requirement, so I asked the person issuing the applications why it was relevant. The young woman shrugged and replied, "It's the hospitals policy". It would seem illegal for an interviewer to ask an applicant if they are a smoker prior to offering an application. However, the practice does go on. Therefore, be mindful of this topic when you are preparing for an interview.

Drinking coffee or smoking prior to an interview

If you are a smoker, one thing to be aware of is, some interviewers may detect the scents remaining on a person's body or in their clothing, after they smoked a cigar or cigarette. That smell could be a nuisance to the interviewer. In some instances, it could outright offend the interviewer, whereby your chances of employment are eliminated. Being conscious of others sensitivities could prevent you from exuding offensive odors.

When the smell of cigarettes is mild or barely noticeable, I am not as offended as when there is a strong odor. This is especially true when the candidate attempts to mask the smell with perfume or cologne. This only intensifies the scent. A primary concern would be for the employees already on staff. If the employees are in a closet space like cubicles or a single mid-sized office, offensive odors can overpower a room. If in doubt, ask yourself, will the smell of cigars or cigarettes offend the interviewer? As my sister Crystal says, "if in doubt do without'.
The same is true for Coffee. I do not drink Coffee and find the smell offensive. I am quickly put off when I interviewed someone who recently downed a cup of coffee then stands so close I become nauseous. Oddly enough, some coffee drinkers are often surprised when they find out, not all adults drink or enjoy the smell of coffee.

Will your smoke breaks hamper productivity?

Most employers and managers I spoke with stated a loss of productivity due to smoke breaks, was a huge concern. They cited instances where an employee needed four smoke breaks per hour. These breaks accounted for a huge drop in productivity and placed the burden on non-smoking co-workers. The loss in productivity coupled with an increased work load resulted in a decline in coworker moral and an increase in the co-worker frustrations. The employers and managers, who identified concerns about this topic, also said although they had concerns about productivity and employee job satisfaction; they had no reservations about hiring smokers.

Can smoking eliminate you from consideration?

In a word, yes. As I wrote in the beginning of this section, some companies have polices preventing them from hiring applicants with certain vices. I have not found information on the legality of this practice, but it does exist.

I spoke with hiring managers who admitted going out to parking lots ahead of a scheduled interview. They would watch candidate's behavior and would make mental notes that they would document later. They said they would monitor candidates for behaviors like smoking, drinking or other conduct they believe would provide insight into the candidate's personality. While I understand their reasoning, this is not a practice I employ or agree with.

The hiring managers said they would watch to see if the candidate seems overly nervous or paced continually around the parking lot, or if they were heavy smokers. Because insurance rates for smokers are higher for smokers than non-smokers, some employers may exclude you if they believe their insurance costs will go up after hiring you. I have not applied this belief and find that the costs associated with smokers was minimal and did not warrant scrutinizing a person's vices. However, some employers may do so and being conscious of that fact could be the difference in getting a position and not being hired.

Will your perfume or cologne offend the interviewer?

Certain types of cologne or perfumes may offend the interviewer. I participated in a panel interview once. One candidate was wearing musk cologne. If you never smelled this type of cologne, I must say, musk cologne has a very strong and somewhat powerful smell. One woman on the panel was pregnant and the smell of the candidate's cologne made her very ill. She was unable to continue the interview and spent a considerable amount of time in the ladies room. Her absences prevented us from continuing his interview and the candidate was asked to leave.

The scent of his cologne lingered for some time. We were forced to open the office windows so fresh air could come in. In all, it took more than 15 minutes to clear the scent of the cologne. An important note to this story is, the candidate's cologne offended one of the interviewers, and caused her to become ill. Her illness delayed the interviews of other candidates. With this in mind, if you must wear perfume or cologne to an interview, always use them in moderation.

Will your fragrance remind the interviewer of someone?

The scent of a particular cologne or perfume could remind the interviewer of someone in his or her past. Remember, this could be a double edged sword. If the memories were positive, then no worries, your interview would go on and you may even receive a positive assessment. However, if your perfume or cologne invokes negative memories, then it is likely to have an adverse effect on the interview, and the interview may not produce positive results.

A thought to consider; over use of colognes and perfumes, prior to an interview, could result in a less than desired reaction. Additionally, your cologne or perfume may open the door for an interviewer to slip in an illegal question. The interviewer may say, "I like your perfume, my husband wears the same kind. Do you mind if I ask where you got it? I would like to buy him some more". If your wife or kids purchased the cologne and you reply, "My wife purchased it for me". If you say something along this line, you have provided the interviewer with some unnecessary personal information. The answer you gave could be used against you and negatively impact your interview. As I wrote earlier, if you must wear colognes or perfumes, always use them in moderation.

Hygiene & grooming
Shower

Most of us would think this is something which does not need to be addressed. However, I had the misfortune of interviewing candidates that had not given their hygienic needs enough attention. In an effort to avoid delving too deep into this topic, it is recommended that proper hygiene is considered and addressed prior to an interview.

Shave

In some industries facial hair has few regulations. Industries in forestry, construction, and some computer related fields may have little concern for the neatness or appearance of facial hair. However, some industries like food service or sales may have stringent standards as it relates to facial hair. Additionally, administrative, managerial, and executive positions may have similarly stringent standards.

If you are interviewing for a position it is important to understanding the organization's position as it relates to this issue. Some positions may require the use of additionally hair nets, as a matter of safety for you and the organization's customers or clients. Some employers may be put off by excessive facial hair, especially if the facial hair is not neatly trimmed or looks as if it has not been attended to in sometime. If you prefer having facial hair, it is a good idea to trim the edges of you facial hair and cut it to an even level so that it appears well kept.

Sit, Relax, and Stay a While

The interview process is a tense time. So try to arrive for the interview a little early. You could use the extra time to compose yourself. As I wrote earlier in the book, the interview process is a stressful time for the interviewer as well. If you have a relaxing mechanism, it may be a good time to employ that mechanism. I enjoy listening to music at a low level when I am trying to relaxing. For some people, a stress ball or chewing gum helps. Just remember to put away your stress ball and discard any gum prior to greeting the interviewer.

Take all appointments off of your calendar

It is extremely important to allow enough time for the interview. If you have an 11:00 AM appointment, scheduling another appointment for 11:45 AM may cause you to miss the second appointment. Additionally, the second appointment may limit your ability to concentrate on your current appointment. If you are distracted, you could rush your answers or not fully comprehend questions and answer questions in a manner which would result in exclusion from further consideration.

Be prepared to pay parking fees

If there are no assigned parking spaces for the organization, it would be a good idea to have a few dollars to cover parking fees. Some companies validate parking. Therefore, the cost of parking would be covered. Nevertheless, it would be a good idea to check for parking a day or so prior to the interview. By doing this, you would know what fees, if any, would be due, along with any time limits associated with those costs.

Plan your route

It is generally a good idea to be prepared to arrive for an interview a few minutes ahead of time to compose yourself. To do this, it is suggested that you are prepared for any delays that you might encounter along your route. This is especially relevant if your interview is in an area that you are not familiar with.

When traveling to an interview that is in an unfamiliar area, it might be a good idea to drive to the location, to time your trip. Also, you could look up the location on the internet. Some sites provide maps and turn by turn directions. By doing this you could ease some of your pre-interview tension, and recognize any potential roadblocks that would hinder you from arriving on time. One way streets and road construction are two such obstructions that you could very well encounter if you fail to preplan your route.

Lastly, I also suggest watching the morning news. The morning news is an excellent source for persons seeking information about road and traffic conditions. The traffic report updates frequently throughout the morning, and will make you aware of any delays that could affect your arrival time.

Negative Statements

As an employer, I am always amazed by the statements of candidates. I have interviewed candidates that were highly critical of their current and former employers. In most situations, these candidates were so critical; I had to interrupt them and explain how concerned I was for their ability to accept organizational changes. I would go on to explain that I was also concerned that if they were that critical of former employers, then they would very likely bring that same temperament to my organization. I would close by explaining my concern of how much of their negative observations for the organization was a result of their actions.

Could negativity eliminate you from consideration?

Negative statements about former employers, places of residence or co-workers could definitely have an adverse effect on your ability to acquire a position. Many employers I discussed this topic with expressed the following concerns:
- Would the candidate cause a decline in employee moral
- Would the candidate openly complain about changes in the organization's policy's and procedure's
- Would the candidate fit into the organization and get along well with managers and co-workers
- Would the candidate bring additional baggage which would cause a reduction in productivity

- Would the candidate be an employee that would constantly disregard the organizations chain-of-command and voice their complaints to persons with little ability to address their issues
- Could the candidate take responsibility for their actions

Most of my colleague's agree that candidates that were overly negative would become employees that were overly negative. These candidates would likely lower employee moral with constant confrontations with their coworkers and the organizations management team. Additionally, these candidates were likely to openly complain about organizational changes with questions like "why is this necessary, everything was ok as they were". My colleague's also had strong beliefs that these candidates were highly likely to create a grapevine that would be ripe with false and counter-productive information. Therefore, during the interview, it would be wise to refrain from any negative language about former coworkers or supervisors.

If I could offer this advice, as the old saying goes, if you cannot say something positive, then do not say anything.

Ask yourself did your statements send the following messages

You do not take accountability for your actions or errors

As an employer, the most frustrating type of employee is the ones that will not take responsibility for their actions. I had an employee that was caught using an organization's vehicle for personal errands. When I confronted the employee, the blame was placed on the supervisors, on coworkers and on the organization policies. The employee spent more than 18 minutes outlining how the organization's culture allowed them to do things which were in direct conflict with the organization's policies. Unfortunately, the employee did not and would not take responsibility for their actions.

During the interview, if a past negative occurrence is uncovered it may be better to acknowledge the event, take responsibility for it and explain how you have made improvement which would prevent future mishaps or mistakes. Failing to acknowledge those discovered mishaps, could cause the interviewer to believe you are not trustworthy. This could also lead them to believe you may bring negative attention to their organization or be a confrontational coworker and employee.

You may not work well with others

As an employer, I am especially watchful for candidates that may not be a good fit for my organization. When I use the term "good fit", I mean an employee that has little regard for their co-workers safety or personal space, or is unwilling to follow established policies and procedures. I would not want to hire a person that would not work well with other employees, or follow the organizations rules. If my employees are unwilling to work well together or follow our rules, I could experience a decline in productivity and profits.

Stakeholders rarely want to see a drop in profits and employers rarely prefer an employee that would upset the cohesiveness of their organizations.

Lamont Jackson

You may have contempt for authority

One of the very worst scenarios for an employer is having an employee that has a dripping disdain for authority. These types of employees are in almost every organization, and will use anything the managers and supervisors say or do to their own advantage.

They openly challenge decisions, and somehow draw their coworkers into their web of belligerence. Their outward resentment of authority undermines the supervisor's authority and negatively affects productivity. Additionally, their behavior also lowers their coworker's moral and confidence in the organization.

At times there seems to be no end to the lengths that these employees will go to disrupt productivity. Most will say or do almost anything. They will claim that they could provide better work environments if they were in charge. Some will even guarantee that they could improve long standing productive procedures.

While these employees can declare that they are better suited to manage an organization, in reality, these employees are less likely to make any meaningful improvements if given the opportunity. These employees could have a dozen motives, many of which I may never understand.

Lastly, confrontational employees can easily consume eighty percent of an employer's time. The time an employer is forced to dedicate to countering the negative effects of these employees lessens the amount of time that they could dedicate to managing the organization.

You may become a negative influence in the workplace

As I wrote in earlier parts of the book, interviewers are especially watchful for candidates that could become a disruptive influence in the workplace. Interviewers are responsible for screening candidates to ensure the best available candidate is hired for a position. Unfortunately, the interviewing process is not an exact science.

There are applicants that meet the requirements of a posted position, perform well during the screening process, and interview well. However, because the interview process is not an exact science, some bad applicants are hired.

As an employee I am sure everyone can recall a person that was an absolute terror to deal with. As a coworker, you might have noticed a number of bad statements or odd behaviors that caused you to distance yourself from that person.

If you can remember a coworker like this, then it is reasonable to assume that the interviewer could also. Employers use various screening processes, as a means to discover the most qualified applicant for a position. Yet, disruptive employees somehow find a way past the screening process and will enter the workplace. Therefore, when the interviewer realizes a candidate could be a negative influence in the workplace they might eliminate them from consideration immediately.

Lamont Jackson

Poor Work History

Work history ranks among the highest of all of the areas that I am especially watchful for. I cannot recall the number of applications I have rejected because of bad work history. If a person is unable to remain at a given job for a steady period of time, I am less likely to give them additional consideration for employment.

Now it is important to understand that it is not very likely every applicant has had a stellar work history or has been able to get along well with every employee or employer that they have encountered. I am a big believer that not every job is right for everyone. However, if I see 5 jobs over a 10 year period and the applicant listed a work history of less than a year on most of the jobs, I am concerned that the applicant may be a disruptive, confrontational or unstable employee. If the employee is unstable, meaning they are not willing to or are unable to remain in any position, I am concerned that they may only remain with my organization only long enough to find another position.

Many of my colleagues echo my concern with regard to this topic. It costs an incredible amount of money and work hours to post job positions, scan applications, schedule and conduct interviews, conduct background, credit and drug and alcohol screenings and to train a candidate. In some industries, this cost could exceed three hundred dollars. When an employee is hired and trained, there is still a learning curve to account for and safety concerns to consider.

With these factors in mind, concerns for an applicant's work history should be understandable. My colleagues have said they are not likely to consider an applicant that they believe would only remain with them for a few months then move on to the next job. This would cause their unemployment cost to rise and the hiring cycle could hamper their organizations productivity for months.

Are there serious issues with your behavior?

When discussing applicants with an unstable poor work history, my colleagues and I wondered, was there an issue with the applicants behavior which cause them to switch jobs so frequently. As I have stated more than once in this book, no employer wants to hire a person that would disrupt their organizations productivity. A behavior question was frequently raised when discussed the work history topic. There were a few areas that we agreed were acceptable causes for employment changes.

- Lay offs
- Relocations
- Unexpected illnesses
- Organization's that closed
- Factories that closed
- Jobs being reassigned to another state or location

Are you able to perform your assigned duties?

Some employers I spoke with explained that they are sometimes apprehensive about hiring a person with poor work history. The points discussed, centered on an applicant's ability to perform assigned tasks. Primarily, was the applicant unwilling to perform a task, or were they unable to do so? If the applicant was unable to perform a task, then it was understandable, as not every position is suited for every person. However, being unwilling to perform a task to standard was not. The common thought was, perhaps the applicant was released from a position due to their inability or unwillingness to perform their jobs at an acceptable level.

Frequent job changes could cause employers to view your abilities as the cause. This could cause the employers to eliminate you from consideration as they might be less interested in taking a chance on you.

Poor Credit History

Depending on your field, the potential for theft could be extremely high. Employers are always concerned about theft. While they may be concerned about theft from outside sources, the threat from within their organizations could carry more significance. In some positions you could have access to sensitive information. This information could be customer and client's personal information, like bank account information or Social Security Numbers. It discredits an employer's organization if an employee uses this information for personal gain.

Theft of personal information is one aspect of an employer's concern. However, employers are also concerned about corporate espionage. Companies constantly work towards gaining an advantage in the market place. Could you imagine what would happen to the Pepsi Corporation if their sensitive information were leaked to a competitor like Coca Cola or Snapple?

If your credit rating is a factor of employment, these issues are likely reasons. Remember, the employer may view your credit as an indicator of potential thefts. However, The U.S. Equal Employment Opportunity Commission's lists the following information, on its website, with regard to Pre-Employment Inquiries and Credit Rating or Economic Status:

Inquiry into an applicant's current or past assets, liabilities, or credit rating, including bankruptcy or garnishment, refusal or cancellation of bonding, car ownership, rental or ownership of a house, length of residence at an address, charge accounts, furniture ownership, or bank accounts generally should be avoided because they tend to impact more adversely on minorities and females. Exceptions exist if the employer can show that such information is essential to the particular job in question.

Will you Embezzle Company Funds?

If the position is in:

- Manufacturing: you could sell company materials for money or steal company materials for another small business which you own or work for
- Corporate settings like:

Marketing: You could be tempted to steal, sell or give away sensitive information to competitors (Social Security Numbers, Company Banking Information, Marketing strategies)

Sales: You could be tempted to steal, sell or give away sensitive information to competitors. (Sales strategies, Social Security Numbers, Contact information, Sales leads)

New business acquisition: You could be tempted to steal, sell or give away sensitive and confidential information to competitors (Sales Leads, New business acquisition strategies)

Research and development: You could be tempted to steal, sell or give away sensitive and confidential information to competitors. (Products being developed, confidential design information, company owned innovative technologies like recipes or formulas')

- Banks or other financial industry propitiations: You could be tempted to steal or sell customer banking information, money held in the bank.
- Construction: You could be tempted to steal, sell or give away information on upcoming contracts, Client information, Company equipment and or supplies. Client's equipment and or supplies.

Criminal History

I have interviewed a number of candidates that had a misstep in their pasts. I was often amazed by the immense potential of these candidates. Most were outstanding craftsmen and paid an amazing amount of attention to detail. Additionally, they multitasked well and were very accountable. In most instances, the candidate's issues occurred early in life, and they were able to show a solid, proven track record of employment.

If you had a misstep or two in your past, you may be asked to explain discrepancies that appear on a background check. If past negative activities are discovered, ensure that you are prepared to address those activities with the interviewer. In most situations, if you are asked to an interview, there was something about your application and resume that captured the interviewer's attention. Therefore, if you are applying for employment, you have already taken a step in the right direction.

One thing to be aware of is you may not receive an offer of employment on many of the interviews you are asked to attend. Some companies have policies in place which prevent them from hiring a candidate with certain offenses on their background check. In most cases, the biggest disqualifier is a felony conviction. However, not all companies have policies against hiring persons with felonies or misdemeanors on their records. If you understand why some companies have policies, you could have a brighter outlook on job hunting.

In some cases, companies may have a policy of exclusion due to past run-ins with persons who were less than model employees. Some employers may have experienced thefts, aggressive behavior or even clients that left the company because one of the employer's candidates has an offense on his or her record. However, it is also important to understand that there are a lot of companies that are willing to take a chance on you. If you encounter one of these companies, please keep future employees in mind. If the employer has a negative experience dealing with you, then it would be understandable if he or she would pass on the next candidate with a background that is similar to yours.

While I cannot paint a rosy picture if you have a conviction on your record, I can say that it is not the end of the world. In some industries, your background and convictions may not eliminate you from consideration. Just be mindful that a rejection is not a personal failure on your part. The employer may simply be limited by company policy. You may hear 20 letters saying, "We are not interested" before you receive an offer of employment. But the one off is all that you will need. I would encourage you to continue applying for employment.

Lastly, some states have enacted a new law to have the criminal history section removed from the employment applications. This law, called "Ban the Box", will apply to state, public and private employers. The National Employment Law Project (NELP) suggests, some US cities have enacted "Ban the Box laws". This law is intended to reduce barriers to the employment of applicants with criminal records. Therefore, employers in cities with Ban the Box laws will no longer be able to use the criminal history section of an application as a single method of eliminating candidates.

For more information and for a list of the growing number of employers who are required to adhere to this law, and the states that have enacted the "Ban the Box" law, go to: http://bantheboxcampaign.org/

Be honest

Most applications ask the question, have you ever been convicted of a crime. It is important to tell the truth. It is against the law to lie about this issue. If you have had a conviction, be sure to explain the conviction if asked. Also, share any treatments you received in connection with any jail or prison time served. Completing anger management counseling or any drug and alcohol counseling courses could cause the interviewer to lower his or her guard. Sharing information about self-improvement programs you completed could be the difference between you and another candidate receiving employment.

Slang and Jargon

There are acronyms, word, terms, or phrases used in the workplace that may be specific to a given industry. These words and terms are classified as jargon, and if at all possible It would be a good idea to limit the use such terms during the interview. Using unrecognizable words or terms rarely impresses an interviewer.

When I was in the U.S. Army, I was in a transportation platoon. During a training session, I was told that we would be doing a road march. I was instructed to have all of my soldiers arrive at midnight, and wearing all of their field gear. When we arrived, there were 6 trucks in a row waiting to transport us. Being a former Marine, this excited me. I assumed we were going to ride out about 30 miles and walk back to base. To my dismay, we rode around for 2 hours then were dropped off at the motor pool. I was extremely upset. I asked why we were back at base before we started a road march. Surprised, one of my soldiers looked at me and said "what do you mean? We just finished it". Apparently, the term "road march", in the US ARMY, meant a ride on a truck, in formation, for a designated amount of time. However, when I was in the U.S. Marines, the term "road march" held the same meaning as the word "hump", which meant we were going to put on our field gear and perform a strenuous walk (for a very long distance at a very swift pace).

This is just an example of how you can never truly know if another person understands every word or term that you use. Likewise, you could offend the interviewer by using a term that you believe means one thing and the interviewer has a completely different definition or assumption of the word or term. Remember, confusion caused by using slang or jargon could result in a misunderstanding which could eliminate you from consideration. Therefore, it is a good idea to only use clear understandable words and terms.

PART IV

The Interview

Traditionally, the interview process was conducted between two individuals, and applicant and a human resources person. However, organizations are using different methods to screen and evaluate applicants. One of these interview methods involves two or more interviewer, commonly called a panel interview. Organizations also conduct group interviews where they interview 3 or more applicants at the same time in the same room. Lastly, a growing number of organizations are using behavioral interviews, where an applicant's ability is evaluated based on a set of situations created by the organization. An explanation of these interviews follows.

Group Interview

In group interviews, a number of applicants, generally 3 or more are invited to interview for a position. In some situations, a team exercise or team building exercise will be conducted. When this occurs, the group interview can be an excellent opportunity for an employer to assess applicants speaking abilities as well as their ability to work within a team.

Group interviews are also a method organizations use to evaluate multiple candidates. By doing this the organization reduces their selection time. The organization might have a high number of qualified candidates, and would like to narrow their choices down to a small and more managcable number. Also, interviewing multiple candidates allows organizations an opportunity to hire an applicant, and select a number of other applicants for positions which could become available at a later date.

Behavioral and Situational Interview

Organizations are beginning to use behavioral and situational interviews more often than the one on one interview. Behavioral and situational interviews are generally used to evaluate an applicant's ability to properly handle a specific set of situations. The interviewer usually asks the applicant questions which places them in a specific situation. Their questions are intended to reveal how an applicant would handle that particular situation. A examples of these types of questions follows:
- Have you ever been a part of a team where someone was did not perform their fair share of the project? **Follow-up question**: How did you handle it?
- Have you had a situation where a co-worker did something that was against the organizations policy? **Follow-up question**: How did you handle it?
- Can you describe a time when your work was criticized?
- Tell me about a time when you had to give someone difficult feedback. How did you handle it?

I use a two person interview system, and add a number of behavioral questions within the interview. This allows me an opportunity to evaluate the applicant's ability to handle a job specific situation.

Panel Interview

The panel interview, of all interview methods, is probably where you will be scrutinized the most. Generally, individuals in the higher income range are interviewed under this method. However, all income levels could be asked to participate in a panel interview. The panel is usually made up of the organizations key stakeholders.

The various panel members will observe and scrutinize everything about you from the moment that your application or resume is submitted, to the time that you exit the room. They will dissect every answer that you provide as well as observe and judge how you interact with members of the panel. Additionally, your mannerisms, attire and ability to answer their questions under these stressful conditions will be assessed and used to determine if you are the most qualified or best fit for the position.

To successfully complete a panel interview, it is always a good idea to arrive early, and be composed in when answering questions. During the interview, remember to relax, and engage the panel directly. Make good eye contact, and when asked a question, if you begin your answer by speaking directly to the person that asked the question, then gradually speak to the panel as a whole, this could help you to relax.

While a panel interview may be very intimidating, it is important to remember that you would not be in the room if you were not qualified and if the organization were not interested. With this in mind, relaxing and answering the questions logically and truthfully could calm the interview jitters.

Skype Interview

Organizations have taken advantage of recent technological advancements to address their staffing needs. Sites like Skype and Go to Meetings have expanded employer's ability to interview and hire future employees. Now, when a position is posted, employers can conduct interviews more efficiently. Applicants, for organizations that use sites like Skype, are no longer required to travel great distances to participate in interviews. Using Skype saves applicants money, especially those applicants that are from another city.

Here are a few suggestions for anyone participating in a Skype interview:
- Position yourself in an uncluttered area
- If possible use a backdrop that is non distracting
- Try to avoid areas has obscene or profane objects
- If you are home, ensure that you have a good internet connection
- If you are at a place that offers free WIFI, try to sit in an area that is as quite as possible. A library might be the best place to do this. Many libraries allow you to reserve rooms on a first come first serve basis.

Every question could have a hidden meaning

My colleagues have said there is a hidden meaning behind many questions they ask. They asked questions geared towards accessing information about your ability to perform a job, or your willingness to accept organizational changes. As a candidate for a position you should remember, there are certain questions that an employer cannot ask you. This topic will be covered in a later chapter. However, interview questions are intended to help the interviewer access you and your ability to fit into their organization and your ability to complete a task. Interviewers should refrain from asking questions about your personal beliefs and practices, race religion, family size and other factors not related to the position.

I use a simple scripted question list, when interviewing applicants. These questions are intended to assist me in acquiring as much information as possible about the applicant's skills and abilities. I created a set of questions for each position, and I use the same questions for every applicant. This allows me to evaluate all applicants equally.

Some employers have created questions which are intended to bring out a certain response from their applicants. Their questions are generally intended to assess the applicant's skills and abilities. While some questions may seem straight forward, the interviewers are able to extract additional information from the answers you provide. Your answer to a question like tell me about yourself, would give the interviewer information about you that they are legally unable to ask. (See the Illegal Questions section of this book for more information)

Why interviewers use complicated questions

Most interviewers ask questions which offer applicants an opportunity to clarify their experience, ability, potential and shortcomings. To some degree, it may be impossible to completely gauge an applicant's abilities during the interview process. However, the questions asked by interviewers will provide some evidence of the strengths and weaknesses of an applicant. Generally your answers say a lot about you. The answers you provide allows the hiring professional to assess your skills and abilities, as well as your ability to express following:
- Are you able to explain your employment history
    - If you are unable to explain your employment history adequately, it could cause the interviewer to doubt you and the information listed on your resume or application.
    - Will your explanation include negative answers about your previous employer? (covered earlier in this book)
- Are you able to clarify your answers if follow-up questions are asked by the interviewer?
    - **Example**: **Question:** What would you do if you witness a fellow employee stealing? **Your**

answer: I would confront the employee, and then inform the supervisor. **Follow-up question:** So what would you do if you informed the supervisor and the supervisor did not act on this information? Your ability to answer follow-up questions as well as the answer that you provide will be used as part of the interviewer's assessment.

- Did you react well when asked difficult questions?
  - Most interviewers understand your nervousness. However, your ability to answer questions adequately might be a vital part of the position that you are applying for. Therefore, if you are applying for a customer service position, there may be times that you are confronted with difficult questions. Your ability to answer those customer questions, complaints or concerns could be the determining factor in you being given further consideration employment, or you being eliminated from consideration

Most interviewers have a very short window to fill empty positions. Therefore, using complicated or dual meaning questions allows the interviewer to assess all selected applicants. After which, the interviewer can reduce the list of applicants down to those they deem to be either the most qualified or best fit for an open position.

Hidden meanings behind interview questions

My college professor used to say, all interview questions are loaded. He would detail how employers would use questions to gain insight into an applicant's personality. In my experience, this is a true statement. It seems all questions asked in an interview holds hidden meanings.

Here are few common question asked during an interview and the intent behind them:

Tell me about yourself

This is a question where the average applicant will give more information than necessary. In my experience, most applicants answered this question with personal information like their date of birth or fraternal affiliations. The information they provided ranged from the number of kids they had to injuries they suffered and family medical information. As an employer, I am not allowed to ask questions about most of these areas. Most of the information provided when answering this question is rarely job related. Therefore, as a reminder, when asked this question, it could be a good idea to confine your answers to only the things about yourself which applied to the job.

In answering this question, you could reply "I have been in this industry for blank years, I have performed blank tasks, and I have worked for X, Y, and Z companies". By only providing information relevant to the job, you eliminate the possibility of the interviewer's pet peeves becoming a factor in the hiring process.

Tell me about a project you were unable to complete and why?

This is meant to see many things. Will the candidate take responsibility for his or her actions during the failed project, or will they pass blame and be overly critical of co-workers, team members and supervisors. If the candidate is willing to express the true cause of the failed project, it says they may be a trustworthy employee or can take a failed project and learn from it.

Tell me about some of your weaknesses.

I am always amazed when I ask this question. Most candidates reply, I have no weaknesses. I often grin, because we all have shortcoming. When asked this question, you do not want to eliminate yourself from consideration, but you do want to share your weaknesses. By all means you should be honest. When answering this question, there are some positive weaknesses like constantly working long hours or will work on job no matter the hour until it is complete.

A candidate once answered this question by saying, "I can't take criticism well". When I asked the candidate to expound on that statement, the candidate went on to say "I get really upset, I like to do things my way, and when I am corrected, I tend to take it personally". While I applauded the candidate's honesty, I was not able to make an offer of employment. Candidates answer lead me to believe the candidate would not be a good fit for my organization.

My college professor once said, he replies to questions about weaknesses with the following statement: "I have a habit of working longer than I should on a project. I will stay after hours to get the job done. I often remain on the job as long as it takes". Now I will say that if anyone does say something like this, it should be the truth. If you are hired, the employer would likely expect this type of effort from you and if you are not willing to match your words with effort, then you could very likely find yourself interviewing for another position.

One example could be:

- I sometimes work long past the end of regular business hours

Tell me about some of your strengths.

This is the question that allows you to share the things about yourself that would be a benefit to the organization. Once again, be sure that you are honest and only share the strength's you actually have and not some you dreamed up on your way to the interview.

A few examples could be:
- I am very meticulous
- I am a self-starter
- I am trainable
- I am dependable

Illegal Question's

Why Personal Questions are Illegal

Federal laws have been established to ensure employers only ask questions that are related to the job they are offering. Any question about a candidate's personal information is considered illegal by both state and federal law.

The Department of Labor has established a number of questions that could provide information which would cause an interviewer to become biased against you. If a person does not like kids or is a member of an opposing political party, this could negatively impact your employment opportunity. Likewise, it could prejudice the interviewer. If you tell an interviewer that you were a Republican and supports a particular Presidents position of a hot button issue, and the interviewer opposes the President or the issue, you could be eliminated from consideration.

The Federal and State laws have leveled the "playing field" so to speak. A candidate cannot be asked about anything which would not have some relation to the open position of the organization.

Sample Illegal Questions

Questions which should not be asked during an interview

Questions about your children:
- Do you have kids?
- How many kids do you have?

Questions about your age:
- How old are you
- When were you born

Questions about your political affiliation:
- What political organizations do you belong to or support

Questions about your religion:
- Are you a Catholic?
- What Church do you belong to?

Questions about your spouse:
- Does your spouse support your career choice?
- How long have you been married

Questions about your physical makeup:
- How tall are you?
- How much do you weigh

Questions with no job relevance:
- What type of car do you drive?

Any question about you sexual preferences, ethnic background, disabilities, age, race religion, marital status or county you were born in are considered illegal. For more information about this topic, please go to:
- http://www.eeoc.gov/laws/practices/index.cfm

Sample Interview Questions

In most cases, one of the most unsettling things about the interview is the fear of the unknown. When an applicant enters the room and the interview begins, it's only natural to have a fear of unknown questions. Questions can race through your mind all night causing you to miss needed hours of sleep. Applicants wonder; will they ask about my background? If they do, what will they want to know? What is the best way to say it? How can I answer the questions and not sound incompetent?

I am sure everyone reading this book is confident in their ability to articulate their background and experiences. However, having concerns about which questions an interviewer may ask or what's the best way to answer the questions is only normal. To assist you with your preparation, I have listed some common questions which my colleagues and I use.

A few questions you may be asked during the interview are:
- Tell Me about yourself
- Why did you leave your last position
- Why should I hire you- I asked a candidate this question once, and the reply was quite unexpected and surprisingly good. The candidate replied, because I would be great for the organization.
- What are your salary requirements
- How do you feel about coworkers that do not pull their share of the work load
- What are some of your weaknesses
- What are some of your strengths
- Describe your style of management
- Do you have any questions
- Describe a project you completed
- Describe a project you could not complete and why
- Describe a time you were confronted about poor work performance and how did you feel
- How would you deal with an unhappy customer
- How would you handle it if your supervisor asked you to perform a task that you did not believe was necessary
- Describe your customer service philosophy
- What is your position on work place safety what is your safety rating

Lamont Jackson

The Information Age

The information age has brought many challenges to small and large business alike. Internet security is a hot issue and organization's spends thousands of dollars protecting their information from outside sources. Organizations also spend a lot of money researching their applicants. The have third party search firms, head hunters and background investigative Company's at their disposal. Yet with all of these paid services in their research tool box, companies can reply on their applicants to provide information that could elude most investigators.

Most applicants do not understand the power of social networks. They place photos of their family, friends, activities as well as their personal, political and religious beliefs on these sites. This information is sitting like an open window for an employer to simply open and gain access to everything about you. Many people believe if they set their status to private for only family and friends, then no outside social media searchers could access it. Unfortunately, this may not be accurate. If one of your friends has a non-private account, an employer could view your information on some sites through their profile.

Your information could then be used for consideration when the employers are making a hiring decision. With that stated, you should be mindful of the information you place in an area that could be used to impact your employment opportunities. This is especially true if you have profanity laced comments all over your site or if your friends seem to used uncomfortable language or views as it could also have an effect on your employment opportunities.

I have met with candidate who expressed concern because they were eliminated because of information on their social network site. If I could offer a piece of advice, be mindful of any information you place on social networks. A photo, a statement or your status could be available years after you have forgotten them. If the information presents a negative image, it could be the difference maker for a finicky employer.

A Few Interview Do's and Don'ts

Sell yourself without over selling yourself. Simply put, take the time to highlight your experience and background. Share how you could be an assist to the organization if hired. There are a few traits I admire in candidates, they include:
- Good team players
- Multi-task's well
- Ability to work well independently
- Works well in groups
- Works well with others
- Dedicated
- Follows directions well
- Accepts criticism and corrects issues quickly

As I stated earlier in the book, when applicants express these things about themselves, I will certainly look a little deeper. Remember however, do not state you have any ability or are willing to perform any task unless you are willing to back it up. Lying during the interview may help you initially but your past has a funny way of popping up at the very worst time. The lie you tell during the interview will definitely be uncovered during the background investigation and that will eliminate you from consideration with the employer as well as the employer's network.

Handshake

This is simple, DO NOT TRY TO BREAK THE INTERVIEWERS FINGERS!!! Just give a SLIGHT amount of pressure and LET GO. I cannot count the number of handshakes that left my hand completely numb for almost 10 minutes. I cannot speak for all employers, but a firm handshake may work well, as long as you are not trying to prove your manhood at the time. You should remember, the interviewers are usually not impressed by this (but some may be) so just be mindful of this.

Greet the interviewer

As a matter of courtesy, if you are sitting when the interviewer walks in it would be a good idea to stand and greet them. This would probably seem fairly obvious to most of use, however, there have been times when applicants neither stood nor acknowledge me or the members of my staff when we entered the room. It really upset the women in the group. The men were unnerved as they believed the candidates were not interested in the position and showed signs of problems that could occur later. In those cases, the candidates were not offered a position. You can never tell what an interviewer reads into your behavior and non-verbal communications. I am not saying be a saint in the interview room. But it is always a good idea to remain mindful of good office etiquette and protocol.

Turn off Your Cellular Phone

This is another area that needs little explanation. Place your cell phone on silent, or turn it off, during the interview. That's it. If you have a ring tone, be careful. You may not want it going off especially if it could offend someone.

During an interview, a candidate's phone went off and the words used in the ring tone made me very uncomfortable, and I served in the U.S. Marines for 4 years and the U.S. Army for 9 years and during my time in the military, I have heard some very racy language. So when it comes to cell phones and ring tones, be mindful and be careful. Simply stated, turn it off.

Cell phones can be a major distraction when it rings. This is especially true if it occurs during the interview. I strongly suggest that you turn off your cell phone until the interview ends

Bring an extra copy of your resume

As I stated earlier in the book, having a sheet of paper with your work history can be a good reference. I find it acceptable for a person to have a few notes that they could refer to about past work experience. Other employers may find it perfectly acceptable to have your resume with you and allow you to review it when answering their questions.

It may be helpful to have an extra copy for the interviewer. The interviewer may have misplaced or not brought their copy to the interview. Having an extra copy of your resume is always a good suggestion.

Make Eye Contact

Having good eye contact with the interviewer is always important. If you do not maintain good eye contact, it could be a sign that you are hiding something. Additionally, failing to maintain good eye contact could be interpreted as a sign of low self-confidence. While low self-confidence is might not be a reason to eliminate an applicant from consideration, it could be a slight concern for some employers. Depending on the industry or position, a certain level of confidence may be necessary. Certain criminal justice professions are an example.

In this particular industry, you may encounter individuals with strong personalities. If these individuals assume that you lack a certain level of confidence, it could cause them to become more aggressive. Once these individuals become aggressive, it would limit your ability to perform you duties. In the criminal justice industry, having a reasonably high level of self-confidence is an important component of the profession.

The food service industry is another area where a fair amount of self-confidence is needed. Often times, an employee in this industry might interact with aggressive customers, who are highly critical. These highly critical individuals have a way of steamrolling individuals that they believe are a bit more timid than usual. Usually, these types of customers are having a bad day, and pour their frustrations onto the food service employee. In this type of situation, the employee is rarely the problem, and should not take the customers criticism personally.

With this in mind, it is important to remember, that being confident can be an asset. However, showing signs of over the top confidence levels could also be a liability. It is important to be yourself. However, it might be a good idea to strike a balance between a decent level of confidence, and a level which could cause you to be perceived as arrogant. Arrogance could negatively impact your employment opportunities. However, here is another point to consider, don't just sit and stare at the interviewer, without breaking eye contact periodically. As funny as it may seem, the interviewer may be just a little uncomfortable if you have a 20 minute interview and never break eye contact.

Good questions to ask an interviewer

I interviewed a candidate once and it was one of the more interesting interviews in recent memory. The candidate had been very cheerful and had a great interview. At the end of the interview, I asked the candidate, do you have any questions for me? The candidate smiled, and using the same cheerful tone that had been used during the interview, said yes, are you going to hire me? Although I could not give an answer at the time, it is an example of how a candidate with a cheerful positive outlook, that interviews well, could have an edge over a competing candidate with similar experience and education.

The following is a list of questions to ask if they were not addressed during the interview:
- If the question about pay was not raised by the end of the interview, it could be a good time to ask about it.
- Are Benefits offered? If so, when
- Is the position full time or part time
- If the position is part time what full time positions may become available
- Does the organization promote from within
- When can I start (I couldn't resist this one) just be careful with this one, some employers may be put off by it. I wouldn't but some might.

I hope this book has been informative and enjoyable. I would like to wish you all good luck in your job search. I'm sure you understand that is impossible to fully outline every situation that you may encounter in an interview. However, my intent was to strengthen your interviewing perspective and interviewing skills, by expressing an employer's perspective. Hopefully, you could recall a few of your past experiences and incorporate the information and techniques from this book to strengthen your interview skills. If you found the information in this book useful, please feel free to comment about the book at my web site. www.lamontjackson.com

Being asked to Multiple Interviews

When I post a position, I will select multiple applicants to interview. I may select six or seven applicants that appear to be the best qualified for the position. I will then review the applications a bit closer, and begin the interview process. If I have not made a decision, after reviewing and interviewing applicants, I may ask the applicants that performed well to return for a second or third interview. This is done to ensure that I can properly access these applicants to ensure that the best person available is selected.

Depending on the position or industry that you are in or applying for, you may be interviewed more than once. If you are asked to return, it usually means that you were successful in completing a specific part of the interview process. During the next interview you may be evaluated more, by a single interviewer or multiple individuals. In some organizations, multiple interviews are required. They conduct multiple interviews to assess applicants or to have applicants conduct various tasks. I once interviewed for a position that was in four parts. There was an initial interview. Individuals that performed well were asked to return and complete an exam, and then we were interviewed by a different member of the Human Resources department. At the third interview the head of the division was in attendance, and at the fourth interview, members of the board of directors were in attendance. Following the final interview, a physical was administered.

I knew a person that turned down an opportunity for a position that paid seventy thousand dollars per year, because they were asked to attend more than one interview. Food for thought, if you are selected and asked to return for another round of interviews, it usually means that the employers believes that you are well suited for a position, and wants to assess your skills and abilities a little closer. It is rarely a bad thing to be asked to interview for a position on more than one occasion.

Lamont Jackson

PART V

Appendix

Additional Information

There are multiple sites available to assist you in your job search. The following list is a brief representation of job resource sites that may assist you with your job search. Good luck and best wishes!!!

Employment Resources
http://www.eeoc.gov/index.cfm
http://www.eeoc.gov/laws/practices/index.cfm

Salary Finders
Mysalary.com
Payscale.com
salarymap.com
Salary.com

Employment Security Commissions
http://www.job-hunt.org/index.html

Federal Job Websites
Fedworld.com
Federalgovernmentjobs.us/search
http://federalgovernmentjobs.us/job-locations.html

Government Job Web Sites
USAjobs.opm.gov
http://www.govtjobs.com/
https://www.governmentjobs.com/ý

Health Care Job Websites
Healthcareweb.com

Medzilla.com
Healthcarejobsite.com
MiracleWorkers.com/Medical_Jobs

Corporate Job Search
Career Builders.com
Monster.com
College grad.com
Blackcollegian.com
HBCU Connect.com
Simplyhired.com
CollegeRecruiter.com
Hotjobs.com
JobFoc.com
Indeed.com
Jobing.com
BilingualCareer.com
CareerPark.com
Dice.com
Snagajob.com
http://www.job-hunt.org/state_unemployment_offices.shtml
http://www.quintcareers.com/top_50_sites.html
http://www.quintcareers.com/general_resources.html

Government Jobs By State

Alabama
http://www.govtjobs.com/state/alabama-government-jobs/
Alaska
http://www.govtjobs.com/state/alaska-government-jobs/
Arizona
http://www.govtjobs.com/state/arizona-government-jobs/

Arkansas
http://www.govtjobs.com/state/arkansas-government-jobs/
California
http://www.govtjobs.com/state/california-government-jobs/
Colorado
http://www.govtjobs.com/state/colorado-government-jobs/
Connecticut
http://www.govtjobs.com/state/connecticut-government-jobs/
Delaware
http://www.govtjobs.com/state/delaware-government-jobs/
D.C.
http://www.govtjobs.com/state/maryland-government-jobs/
Florida
http://www.govtjobs.com/state/floria-government-jobs/
Georgia
http://www.govtjobs.com/state/georgia-government-jobs/
Hawaii
http://www.govtjobs.com/state/hawaii-government-jobs/
Idaho
http://www.govtjobs.com/state/idaho-government-jobs/
Illinois
http://www.govtjobs.com/state/illinois-government-jobs/
Indiana
http://www.govtjobs.com/state/indiana-government-jobs/
Iowa
http://www.govtjobs.com/state/iowa-government-jobs/
Kansas
http://www.govtjobs.com/state/kansas-government-jobs/

Kentucky
http://www.govtjobs.com/state/kentucky-government-jobs/
Louisiana
http://www.govtjobs.com/state/louisiana-government-jobs/
Maine
http://www.govtjobs.com/state/maine-government-jobs/
Maryland
http://www.govtjobs.com/state/maryland-government-jobs/
Massachusetts
http://www.govtjobs.com/state/massachusetts-government-jobs/
Michigan
http://www.govtjobs.com/state/michigan-government-jobs/
Minnesota
http://www.govtjobs.com/state/minnesota-government-jobs/
Mississippi
http://www.govtjobs.com/state/mississippi-government-jobs/
Missouri
http://www.govtjobs.com/state/missouri-government-jobs/
Montana
http://www.govtjobs.com/state/montana-government-jobs/
Nebraska
http://www.govtjobs.com/state/nebraska-government-jobs/
Nevada
http://www.govtjobs.com/state/nevada-government-jobs/
New Hampshire
http://www.govtjobs.com/state/newhampshire-government-jobs/

New Jersey
http://www.govtjobs.com/state/newjersey-government-jobs/
New Mexico
http://www.govtjobs.com/state/newmexico-government-jobs/
New York
http://www.govtjobs.com/state/newyork-government-jobs/
North Carolina
http://www.govtjobs.com/state/northcarolina-government-jobs/
North Dakota
http://www.govtjobs.com/state/northdakota-government-jobs/
Ohio
http://www.govtjobs.com/state/ohio-government-jobs/
Oklahoma
http://www.govtjobs.com/state/oklahoma-government-jobs/
Oregon
http://www.govtjobs.com/state/oregon-government-jobs/
Pennsylvania
http://www.govtjobs.com/state/pennsylvania-government-jobs/
Rhode Island
http://www.govtjobs.com/state/rhodeisland-government-jobs/
South Carolina
http://www.govtjobs.com/state/southcarolina-government-jobs/
South Dakota
http://www.govtjobs.com/state/southdakota-government-jobs/
Tennessee
http://www.govtjobs.com/state/tennessee-government-jobs/

Texas
http://www.govtjobs.com/state/texas-government-jobs/
Utah
http://www.govtjobs.com/state/utah-government-jobs/
Vermont
http://www.govtjobs.com/state/vermont-government-jobs/
Virginia
http://www.govtjobs.com/state/virginia-government-jobs/
Washington
http://www.govtjobs.com/state/washington-government-jobs/
West Virginia
http://www.govtjobs.com/state/westvirginia-government-jobs/
Wisconsin
http://www.govtjobs.com/state/wisconsin-government-jobs/
Wyoming
http://www.govtjobs.com/state/wyoming-government-jobs/

State Employment Sites

Alabama
Department of Industrial Relations
http://labor.alabama.gov/
Department of Labor
http://alalabor.stat.al.us
Personnel Department
http://www.personnel.state.al.us/

Alabama Job Klink
   https://joblink.alabama.gov/ada/mn_offices_dsp.cfm?choice=1&comingfromthemenu=1&rand=898038

Alaska
Alaska Job Center Network
   http://www.jobs.state.ak.us/
Department of Labor and Workforce Development
   http://www.labor.state.ak.us/
Office of Equal Employment Opportunity
   http://www.eeo.state.ak.us

Arizona
Arizona Workforce Connection
   http://www.arizonaworkforceconnection.com/
Human Resources Division
   http://www.hr.state.az.us/
Industrial Commission of Arizona
   http://www.ica.state.az.us/
State Compensation Fund
   www.statefund.com

Arkansas
Arkansas Workforce
   http://dws.arkansas.gov/AWIB/index.htm
Department of Labor
   http://www.labor.ar.gov/Pages/default.aspx
Department of Workforce Education
   http://www.work-ed.state.ar.us/
Employment Security Department
   http://dws.arkansas.gov/
Workers' Compensation Commission
   http://www.awcc.state.ar.us/

California
Cal JOBS
   https://www.caljobs.ca.gov/vosnet/Default.aspx
Department of Fair Employment and Housing

http://www.dfeh.ca.gov/
Department of Industrial Relations
http://www.dir.ca.gov/
Department of Personnel Administration
http://www.calhr.ca.gov/Pages/home.aspx
Employment Development Department
http://www.edd.cahwnet.gov
Employment Training Panel
http://www.etp.cahwnet.gov/
State Personnel Board
http://www.spb.ca.gov/

Colorado
Department of Labor and Employment
http://www.colorado.gov/cs/Satellite/CDLE-Main/CDLE/1240336821467
Department of Personnel and Administration
http://www.state.co.us/dpa/

Connecticut
Department of Labor
http://www.ctdol.state.ct.us/
Workers' Compensation Commission
http://wcc.state.ct.us/

Delaware
Department of Labor
http://www.delawareworks.com/
State Personnel Office
http://delawarepersonnel.com/
Virtual Career Network
http://www.vcnet.net/

Florida
Agency for Workforce Innovation
https://jobs.myflorida.com/index.html
State Jobs
http://www.floridajobs.org/

Georgia
Department of Labor
http://www.dol.state.ga.us/
Georgia Commission on Equal Opportunity
http://gceo.state.ga.us/
State Merit System of Personnel Administration
http://www.gms.state.ga.us/

Hawaii
Department of Human Resources Development
http://dhrd.hawaii.gov/
Department of Labor and Industrial Relations
http://labor.hawaii.gov/

Idaho
Department of Commerce & Labor
http://www.labor.idaho.gov
Idaho Career Information System
http://labor.idaho.gov

Illinois
Department of Employment Security
http://www.ides.illinois.gov/default.aspx
Department of Labor
http://www.illinois.gov/idol/Pages/default.aspx
Illinois Civil Service Commission
http://www2.illinois.gov/icsc/Pages/default.aspx
Illinois Workers' Compensation Commission
http://www.iwcc.il.gov/

Indiana
Department of State Personnel
http://www.in.gov/spd/
Department of Labor
http://www.in.gov/dol/
Department of Workforce Development
http://www.in.gov/dwd/

Iowa
Department of Personnel
   www.state.ia.us/government/idop/index.html
IDED: Iowa The SmartCareer Move
   http://www.iowaeconomicdevelopment.com/BusinessDev/WorkforceTraining
Iowa Jobs
   http://www.iowajobs.org/
Iowa Workforce Development
   http://www.iowaworkforce.org/

Kansas
Department of Labor
   http://www.dol.ks.gov/index.html
Kansas Job Link
   http://ww2.kansasjoblink.com/ada/

Kentucky
Cabinet for Workforce Development
   http://kentuckycareercenter.ky.gov/
Department of Labor
   http://www.labor.ky.gov/Pages/LaborHome.aspx
Department of Personnel
   https://personnel.ky.gov/Pages/default.aspx
Environmental and Public Protection Cabinet
   http://www.environment.ky.gov/
Office of Employment and Training
   http://www.kewes.ky.gov/

Louisiana
Department of Labor
   http://www.laworks.net/
Department of State Civil Service
   http://www.civilservice.louisiana.gov/

Maine
Department of Labor
  http://www.state.me.us/labor/
Department of Labor: CareerCenter
  http://www.mainecareercenter.com/

Maryland
Department of Labor, Licensing and Regulation
  http://www.dllr.state.md.us/

Massachusetts
Division of Employment and Training
  http://www.mass.gov/lwd/

Michigan
Department of Career Development
  http://www.michigan.gov/wda
Department of Civil Service
  http://www.michigan.gov/mdcs
Michigan Works:
  https://www.michworks.org/
Office of the State Employer
  http://www.michigan.gov/ose/

Minnesota
Bureau of Mediation Services
  http://mn.gov/bms/
Department of Economic Security
  http://mn.gov/deed/
Department of Employee Relations
  http://www.sos.state.mn.us/index.aspx?page=772
Department of Employment and Economic Development
  http://mn.gov/deed/
Department of Labor and Industry
  http://www.doli.state.mn.us/
Minnesota's Job Bank
  www.mnworks.org

Lamont Jackson

Mississippi
Department of Employment Security
http://mdes.ms.gov/
Mississippi Job Bank
http://mississippi.us.jobs/
Mississippi Workers' Compensation Commission
http://www.mwcc.state.ms.us/

Missouri
Department of Labor and Industrial Relations:
Unemployment Insurance Tax
http://labor.mo.gov/DES/Employers/
Great Hires
http://jobs.mo.gov/

Montana
Department of Labor and Industry
http://dli.mt.gov/
Montana Job Service
https://jobs.mt.gov/jobs/login.seek

Nebraska
Department of Labor
https://dol.nebraska.gov/

Nevada
Department of Employment, Training and Rehabilitation
http://detr.state.nv.us/
Department of Personnel
http://hr.nv.gov/

New Hampshire
Department of Labor
https://dol.nebraska.gov/
NH WORKS
http://www.nhworks.org/

New Jersey
Department of Labor
    http://lwd.state.nj.us/labor/index.html
Department of Personnel
    http://www.state.nj.us/nj/employ/
Workforce New Jersey Public Information Network
    http://wnjpin.state.nj.us/
New Jersey Civil Service Commission
    http://www.nj.gov/csc/
    http://www.state.nj.us/csc/seekers/jobs/announcements

New Mexico
New Mexico Work Force Connection
    https://www.jobs.state.nm.us/vosnet/Default.aspx
New Mexico Department of Work Force Solutions
    http://www.dws.state.nm.us/

New York
Department of Civil Service
    http://www.cs.ny.gov/

Department of Labor
    http://www.labor.ny.gov/home/
New York State Insurance Fund
    http://ww3.nysif.com/

North Carolina
Department of Commerce: Employment Security Commission
    https://www.ncesc1.com/
Department of Labor
    http://www.nclabor.com/
Office of State Personnel
    http://www.oshr.nc.gov/
North Carolina Office State of Human Resources
    http://www.oshr.nc.gov/

City of Raleigh
   http://www.raleighnc.gov/home/content/Departments/Articles/HumanResources.html

North Dakota
Department of Labor
   http://www.nd.gov/labor/
Job Service North Dakota
   http://www.jobsnd.com/
Workforce Safety & Insurance
   http://www.workforcesafety.com/

Ohio
Bureau of Workers' Compensation
   https://www.bwc.ohio.gov/
Department of Job and Family Services
   http://jfs.ohio.gov/
State Employment Relations Board
   http://www.serb.state.oh.us/

Oklahoma
Department of Labor
   http://www.ok.gov/odol/
Employment Security Commission
   http://www.ok.gov/oesc_web/
Office of Personnel Management
   http://www.ok.gov/OSF/

Oregon
Bureau of Labor and Industries
   http://www.oregon.gov/BOLI/pages/index.aspx
Department of Consumer and Business Services
   http://www.oregon.gov/DCBS/Pages/index.aspx
Employment Department
   http://www.oregon.gov/EMPLOY/Pages/index.aspx
State Jobs Page
   http://www.oregon.gov/jobs/Pages/index.aspx

Pennsylvania
Department of Labor and Industry
http://www.dli.state.pa.us/portal/server.pt/community/l_i_home/5278

Rhode Island
Department of Labor and Training
http://www.dlt.ri.gov/

South Carolina
Employment Security Commission
http://www.sces.org/

South Dakota
Bureau of Personnel
http://bhr.sd.gov/

Tennessee
Department of Labor and Workforce Development
http://www.state.tn.us/labor-wfd/
Department of Personnel
http://www.tn.gov/dohr/

Texas
Texas Rehabilitation Commission
http://www.dars.state.tx.us/

Utah
Department of Human Resource Management
http://www.dhrm.utah.gov/
Department of Workforce Services
http://jobs.utah.gov/
Labor Commission
http://laborcommission.utah.gov/

Vermont
Department of Employment and Training
http://labor.vermont.gov/

Department of Labor and Industry
  http://labor.vermont.gov/
Department of Personnel
  http://www.vermontpersonnel.org/
Labor Relations Board
  http://vlrb.vermont.gov/home

Virginia
Employment Security Commission
  http://www.vec.virginia.gov/
Virginia Workforce Connection
  https://www.vawc.virginia.gov/vosnet/Default.aspx
Department of Human Resource Management
  http://www.dhrm.state.va.us/
Department of Labor and Industry
  http://www.doli.virginia.gov/
Virginia Employment Commission
  http://www.vec.virginia.gov/

Washington
Department of Employment Security
  http://www.esd.wa.gov/
Department of Labor and Industries
  http://www.lni.wa.gov/
Department of Human Resource Management
  http://www.dop.wa.gov/Pages/default.aspx

West Virginia
Workforce Connection of West Virginia
  http://www.wvcommerce.org/business/workforcewv/default.aspx
Division of Labor
  http://www.wvlabor.com/newwebsite/Pages/index.html

Wisconsin
Department of Workforce Development
  http://dwd.wisconsin.gov/

Office of State Employment Relations
   http://oser.state.wi.us/

Wyoming
Department of Employment
   http://wyomingworkforce.org/Pages/default.aspx
Department of Workforce Services
   http://wyomingworkforce.org/Pages/default.aspx
Wyoming Job Network
   https://www.wyomingatwork.com/vosnet/Default.aspx

References

U.S. Equal Employment Opportunity Commission
Prohibited Employment Policies/Practices

http://www.eeoc.gov/laws/practices/index.cfm

http://bantheboxcampaign.org/

About the Author

Lamont Jackson is a General Manager with over 27 years of human resources and management experience. Lamont facilitates a monthly interviewing workshop and has advised members of the local Employment Security Commission branches on hiring and interviewing related topics. This book was written to complement his workshop.

As an entrepreneur, Lamont has managed artist performing in multiple genres including R&B, Christian Rock, Comedy, Gospel and Rap. His clients also included, Actors, Motivational Speakers, Authors as well as Music Producers Independent Record Labels and Production Companies. Lamont is also an Executive Producer for E^3 Entertainment and the CEO of Emont Publishing, Inc. and Wavelength Entertainment Group.

Lamont has been an independent consultant and web designer for 9 years, as well as a workshop facilitator, an author, comedian and motivational speaker.

Lamont is a Gulf War Veteran and has served in the United States Marine Corps and the U.S. Army. Lamont is an alumnus of Saint Augustine's College and holds a Bachelors of Science Degree in Organizational

Management. He is currently pursuing a MBA with Strayer University.

Lamont Jackson

Notes

Lamont Jackson